Frozen Hotels

Isabel Thomas

Contents

 This page is for an adult to read to you.

Mini, Macro and Micro World!

 This page is for an adult to read to you.

Did you know?

Non-fiction books do not have to be read in order – that is, from front to back. The contents page can give you ideas for what to read first.

CODE EXTRA

Frozen Hotels

Isabel Thomas

Contents

OXFORD

Fact!

There are many ice hotels all over cold parts of the world, from Canada to Sweden.

Mini's Top Spot

Can you find this measurement?

1 m

Can you remember what 'm' means?

 This page is for an adult to read with you.

Before you read

Sound checker

Say the sounds.

ge dge g

Tricky words

their
once

Sound spotter

Blend the sounds.

Into the zone

What do you think an ice hotel would be like?

A frosty welcome

This hotel is in Sweden, at the edge of the **Arctic Circle**. It is made from snow and 1000 huge blocks of ice.

Walls of ice

In spring, when the weather gets warm, the ice hotel melts! A new hotel is made every year using ice from a frozen river. It's a hazardous job. The drivers must avoid falling through the ice.

Forklifts heaved the giant ice blocks out of the river.

1 m

Keeping warm

When these people arrived at this ice hotel in Canada, they changed into layers of clothes and put on hats to keep warm. Inside the hotel, it is colder than a fridge!

Brrrrrrrr!

I'm shivering like a j-j-jelly!

Looking around

Once visitors are warm, they can enjoy the hotel. Each door reveals a new surprise. All the **seats** and tables are carved from ice. They sparkle like gems.

Even the cups are made from ice!

Jump on!

It's time to see the sights by **sledge**. Husky dogs have lots of energy. They move quickly across the snow, pulling their passengers towards frozen lakes and forests.

husky dog
I hope this is the right direction!

Time for bed

Visitors sleep on a **ledge** of ice inside large sleeping bags. A fire roars to keep their toes toasty!

Glossary

Arctic Circle — the part of the globe around the North Pole

forklifts — diggers used to lift heavy things

ledge — a flat shelf that sticks out

seats — things people sit on, like chairs

sledge — a thing used to carry people across snow and ice

Index

 This page is for an adult to read with you.

Now you have read ...

Frozen Hotels

Take a closer look

Why do ice hotels have to be built again after every year?
Check back to page 6 if you are not sure.

Thinking time

Would you like to stay in an ice hotel?
Can you explain why or why not?